Where Does The Sky Touch The Ground

(Small Book)

Peter Blueberry

Thank you for the light

of inspiration

Olivia, Blake, Calvin, Dane,

and Rose.

Where Does The Sky Touch The Ground
(Small Book)
© 2019 Peter Blueberry

Library of Congress Control Number: 2017951576

Table of Contents

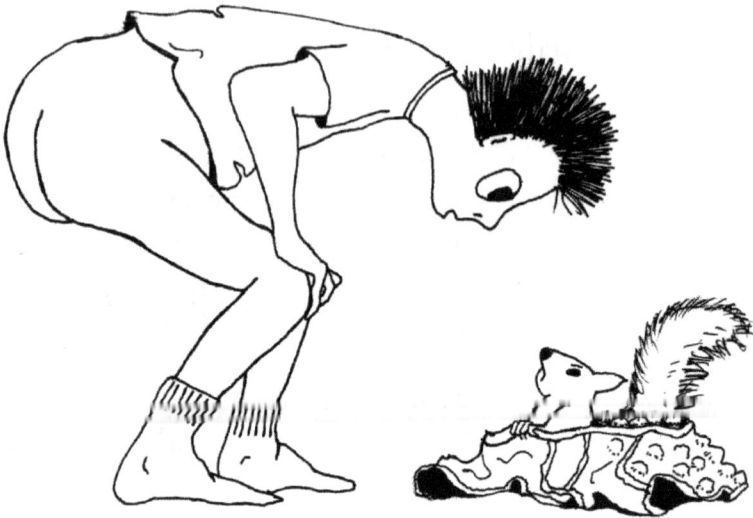

N! O! No!

There's A Squirrel In My Underwear

There's a squirrel in my underwear,
And I can't get him out.
He's storing up his acorns,
And it does no good to shout.

I don't think he's going to leave.
I think he's going to stay.
I think he wants to bite me.
I guess I'll go **without my underwear today.**

The Landing

Monty Guy
Was 20 feet high,
And his legs were long and lean.

When he sat in a chair,
It was quite an affair.
The craziest thing you'd ever seen.

Putting his thumb into gear,
He stuck out his rear,
And peered down from where…
…he was standing.

While taking aim on…
…the seat,
He steadied his feet.
Then sent his rear…
… in for a landing.

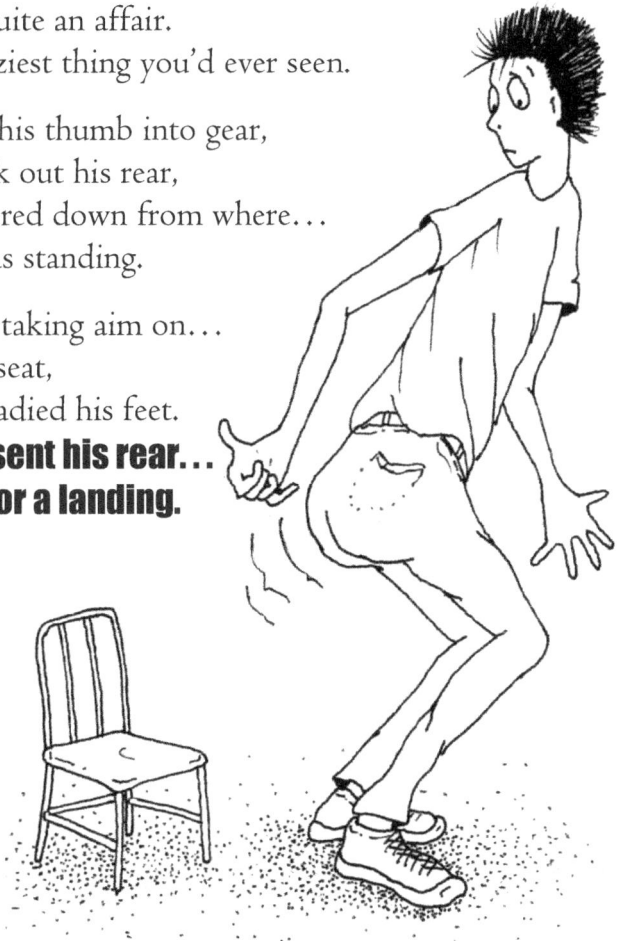

It sure seems small from way up here!

I'll be right here if you need me.

I'd Rather Play With The Box

I got a brand new bike.
It came in a great big box.
My Dad put it together.
It's called a 'Flying Fox'.

He's going to teach me to ride,
But it will take a while to learn.
I'll have to practice a lot.
I'm just a little concerned.

"But it'll be O.K.,"
That's what my Dad said.
But for now can I stay right here,
And **play with the box instead?**

The Egg

Gracie Peg
Tried to fry an egg
Outside on the sidewalk in the sun.

Hot was the air,
And hard to bear.
The temperature was 100 and I.

But, when she cracked the egg.
It grew two legs,
And walked off with a stride.

"After this,"
She said, "I quit.
I'm going to **cook my . . .**
. . . eggs inside."

That's the last time I use double A grade monster eggs!

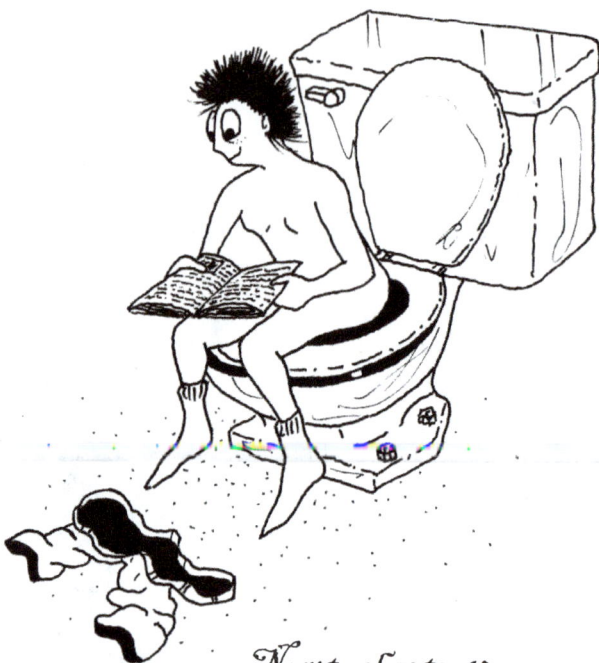

Now to chapter 13.

My Reading Room

I have a special place
Where I like to go and read.
It's so very quiet,
And comfortable to me.

I can sit for hours.
Reading my book for ages.
And quietly flush the toilet,
While I **gently turn the pages**.

Stepping Off A Curb

Stepping off a curb
Is something of a chore.
You better look both ways,
Or you're gona get squished for sure.

There's adventure and excitement,
And it's happening over there.
There's exciting things to do.
You can feel it in the air.

So, I'm going to take a journey,
New adventures I will meet.
And someday I'm going to do it.
As soon as I'm allowed to . . .

. . . cross the street.

One small step for me.
One giant leap for my mom.

Splashing

Puddles are for splashing,
And throwing out your hands.
Puddles are for smashing
As hard as you possibly can.

Puddles get you muddy,
And puddles get you wet,
But I haven't seen a puddle
That I would pass up yet.

I can be a Pirate,
A hundred miles out to sea,
Or I can be a Knight,
And slay a dragon 2 or 3.

But whatever I decide on,
Whatever I want to be,
I just hope it rains enough
To make puddles for Calvin and me .

Crashing

It's quite awesome,
When the sea roars.
Crashing and smashing
Onto the sea's shores.

Water spray exploding.
Shooting into the sky.
What a spectacle it makes
To young watchful eyes.

Beating and pounding
Onto the jagged rocks.
Then thoroughly drenching
The standing wooden docks.

And although it's quite awesome,
What the sea can do,
Just be very careful
That the sea **doesn't get you**.

There's An Elephant In My Bed

There's an elephant in my bed,
And he said he won't get out.
He's eating jelly sandwiches,
And he said he's not about;

To leave the cozy comfort
Of my blankets and my bed.
He said he'll never leave.
Now get that through my head.

So, I'm going to call the zoo police
To hurry and bring a net.
I'll teach the elephant a lesson.
One he's never going to forget.

I'll box his ears and tie up his feet,
So he won't be able to walk.
But don't you think the strangest thing
Is that this elephant can **actually talk.**

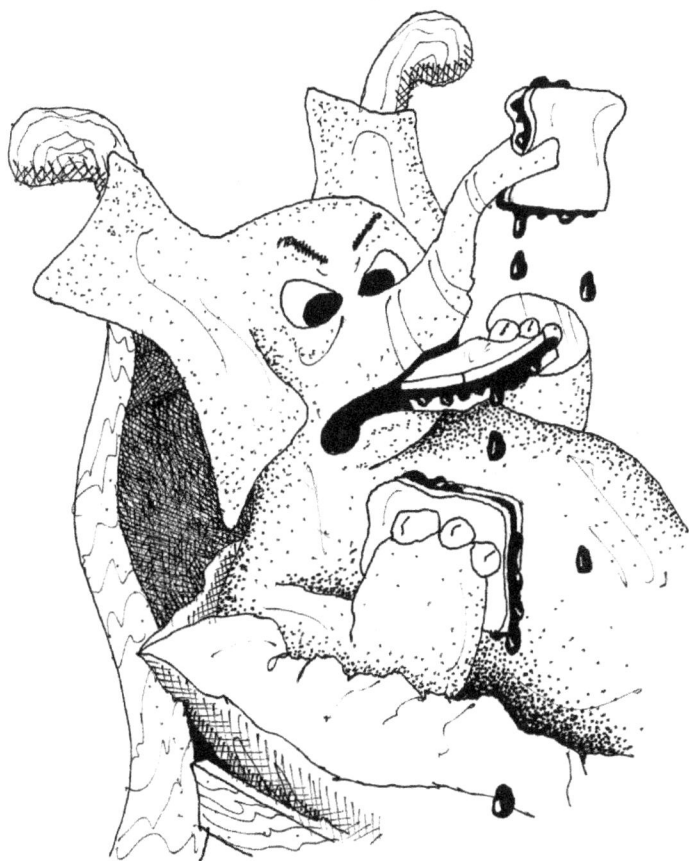

Ahhh. Peanut butter and slime berries.

Where Does The Sky Touch The Ground

Where does the sky
  Touch the ground?
  Please, tell me where
  It needs to be found.

  It's an enchanted land
  Where wisdom abounds,
  Treasures of knowledge,
And gentle grounds.

But it looks to me
  Like it's so far away.
  You couldn't get there
  Not in a day.

  But, I'm going to try
  One of these days.
  When I'm much older,
And wise in my ways.

It's a place
  That needs to be found,
  **Where the sky
  Touches the ground.**

I can see forever and ever, forever!

This is one weird dream.

Homework

I just hate doing homework!
It takes up too much time.
Having fun is good for you.
Having fun is fine.

I'd rather enjoy the sunshine.,
Be outside and play.
It's outside I'd rather be.
It's inside I hate to stay.

So, the solution to my problem,
And it would be so neat,
If I could do my homework
At night **while I'm asleep.**

The String

Today I found a string
Just lying on the ground.
It has a beginning,
But no end can be found.

I wonder where it goes,
And just how far away,
The end is from...
...the beginning.
Could I find it in a day?

Maybe it will lead
To some hidden treasure.
Or maybe at the end
Is some sweetened...
...pleasure.

But I don't have the time.
I hear the school...
...bell sound.
I guess I'll leave the string
Just lying on the ground.

Wow! I wonder who left this here?

Oh! Not this again!

Air Head

Why is your head
Floating in the air?
Did it come off
When you were . . .
. . . brushing your hair?

Or did it come off
When you were . . .
. . . blowing your nose?
Did it become unhitched?
Is that why it rose?

Or was it because
You forgot it was there.
You weren't paying attention.
You just didn't care.

Well, your mother did say
You would lose your head.
If it wasn't screwed on.
That's what she said.

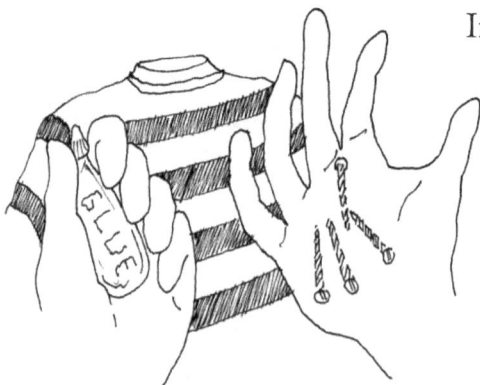

Now, you can't . . .
. . . go around
With no head . . .
. . . upon you.
So, here are . . .
. . . some **screws**,
And here is some **glue**.

The Shower

There was a Hippo who took a shower.
He stayed in there for nearly 4 hours.
He scrubbed and scrubbed and scrubbed his skin.
He scrubbed and scrubbed **until he was thin .**

That was sure invigorating!

I'm waiting.

Tell Me A Story

Tell me a story.
Read me a poem.
Recite a limerick.
I want to enjoy,

A few minutes of your time,
I want of you.
Please, tell me a story.
I'll sit here **till you do.**

Doers And Don'ters

The Doers do,
And the Don'ters don't.
The Doers will do
What the Don'ters won't.

And when the Doers do
What the Don'ters don't,
The Doers have fun
That the Don'ters won't.

Example…

The Doers have fun
Helping someone like you.
If you want to feel good,
Go help someone too.

Which one is the don'ter?

Tooth Fairy Monster

I lost a tooth this morning,
And put it under my pillow,
But when I looked real close,
It was all gunky and yellow.

How can this possibly be?
I brush my teeth at night,
3 times to the left,
And 3 times to the right.

That should be enough.
I have things to do.
That should take care of all
The food I choose to chew.

But maybe that's not enough,
And I should brush them a little longer,
Because what's standing in front of me now,
Is not the Tooth Fairy. . .
. . . but the **Tooth Fairy Monster.**

White teeth – I pay you.
Yellow teeth – We need to talk!
A big talk!

Laaa-Laa
Hjhr

Singing Willy

Willy Sloat
Couldn't hold a note,
But he sang his heart out and tried.

When he went outside
To sing his songs,
People covered their ears and cried.

Then, the people of the village
Said "Hey, Willy.
Why don't you go to the big city and sing?"

"We'll get you a ticket,
And pack your bags.
We'll take care of everything."

So, Willy said, "Yes.
I'll go to the big city."
And he sang his songs everywhere.

And though Willy was different
They said he was 'Unique'.
And soon Willy was a **millionaire.**

It's Magical

Would you like to see some magic?
Drop this seed upon the Earth.
Cover it up with dirt,
But water it first.

Then stand back and watch
The magic start to flow.
From right up out of the Earth
Something will start to show.

A tiny stem appears.
Growing towards the sky.
Budding blossoms into flowers.
What a pleasure to the eye.

The colors that you see;
Yellows, pinks and reds,
Are magically made from dirt
As the blossoming flower spreads,

And the magic will continue
While this living stem grows.
Now, don't you think it's magical
Turning dirt into a rose?

Oh well! Better next time.

I'm In Training

I spill my milk
At every meal.
My food ends . . .
. . . up in my lap.

My clothes are a mess
When I play outside,
And I don't fall . . .
. . . asleep when I nap.

I fall off the toilet
If I sit too long.
And my room is . . .
. . . always a mess.

There's gum in my hair,
Spaghetti up my nose,
And I can't explain the rest.

But, this is the way
It's supposed to be.
So please stop complaining.

You ought to know,
At least by now,
That I am **still in training**.

"I just love my new goggles"

QUESTIONS

4. THERE'S A SQUIRREL IN MY UNDERWEAR

What is the squirrel doing? *Storing up acorns*

   B. What will he have to do? *Go without his underwear today*

5. THE LANDING

   A. How tall was Monty Guy? *20 feet*
   B. What did he send in for a landing? *His rear*

6. I'D RATHER PLAY WITH THE BOX

   A. What kind of a bike was it? *A Flying Fox*
   B. What did she want to do? *Play with the box*

7. THE EGG

   A. How hot was it? *100 and 1*
   B. What happened when she cracked the egg? *It grew two legs and walked off with a stride*

8. MY READING ROOM

   A. Where is he? *On the toilet*

9. STEPPING OFF THE CURB

   A. What can't he do? *Cross the street*

10. SPLASHING

   A. What does he hope for? *Enough rain to make puddles*
   B. How many dragons can he slay? *2 or 3*

12. CRASHING

   A. Where does the sea roar? *At the sea's shore*
   B. What do you have to be careful of? *That the sea doesn't get you*

14. THERE'S AN ELEPHANT IN MY BED

   A. What is the elephant eating? *Jelly sandwiches*
   B. Who is going to be called? *The Zoo Police*

16. WHERE DOES THE SKY TOUCH THE GROUND

   A. Where does the sky touch the ground? *In an enchanted land*
   B. When will he try to find it? *When*

18. HOMEWORK

   A. When does he want to do his homework? *At night when he's asleep*

19. THE STRING

   A. What can't be found? *The end of the string*
   B. Where might the string lead to? *A hidden treasure or some sweetened pleasure*

20. AIR HEAD

   A. What did his Mother say? *You would lose your head if it wasn't screwed on*

21. THE SHOWER

   A. Who was in the shower? *A hippo*
   B. How long did he scrub? *For nearly 4 hours*

22. TELL ME A STORY

   A. How long will he sit there? *Till he's told a story, poem or limerick*

23. DOERS AND DON'TERS

   A. What do Doers do? *What Don'ters don't*

24. TOOTH FAIRY MONSTER

   A. What did his tooth look like? *All gunky and yellow*
   B. Why did the Tooth Fairy Monster show up? *He didn't brush his teeth enough*

26. SINGING WILLY

   A. What did the people do when Willy sang? *They covered their ears and cried*
   B. What did Willy become? *A millionaire*

28. IT'S MAGICAL

   A. What do you put upon the Earth? *A seed*
   B. What starts to show? *A tiny stem*
   C. What is the Rose made from? *Dirt*

30. I'M IN TRAINING

   A. What happens to the milk? *It's spilled at every meal*
   B. What's up his nose? *Spaghetti*